The last years of BR steam aroun

BATH SPA

BATH
GREEN PARK

82F

First published in 2016

British Library Cataloguing in Publication Data

A catalogue record for this book is available from the British Library.

ISBN 978 1 85794 477 8

Silver Link Publishing Ltd
The Trundle
Ringstead Road
Great Addington
Kettering
Northants NN14 4BW

Tel/Fax: 01536 330588
email: sales@nostalgiacollection.com
Website: www.nostalgiacollection.com

Printed and bound in the Czech Republic

Title page main image **MIDFORD:** Standard Class 4 4-6-0 No 75072 pulls away from Midford with the 4.35pm service from Bath Green Park to Templecombe on 22 May 1965.

Title page inset **MIDFORD:** Midford station still looks trim and well cared for in this view taken on 2 June 1963. The station house can be seen above its wooden buildings, as can the station's distinctive 'calling back' signal. My grandfather, Charles Moors, was station master here between 1926 and 1934. During this period he also took charge of Wellow station. Both became unstaffed halts in 1964. *Author*

Contents

Acknowledgements

I would like to thank those who have helped me with this book. Several of them also contributed to my previous publications, including Steve Edge, who has provided the map, while Ian Bennett has again allowed me to use coloured photographs taken by the late M. E. J. Deane. I must also acknowledge the contribution of a former colleague of my late aunt, Edna Moors, who worked for the 'Admiralty' in Bath in the 1960s and with whom I exchanged photographs of the last years of the S&D. Sadly I have no record of his name, and his photos are marked 'Author's collection' in this book. Three photos were taken for me on Saturday 18 August 1962 and are credited to my school friend, Charles Huff. I have also used a number of photographs taken by my late uncle, Denis Horton.

Many of these 'Recollections' are my own, but I have also obtained valuable information about the Somerset & Dorset line from the books of the late Ivo Peters (published by OPC in the early 1980s). Other information has come from contemporary copies of Ian Allan's *Trains Illustrated* and *Modern Railways* magazines. Building and scrapping dates for the various steam engines are from *Hugh Longworth's British Railways Steam Locomotives 1948-1968*, published by OPC in 2005.

The text has benefited from the early proofreading and editing carried out by my wife Susan. Finally I would like to acknowledge the help and encouragement received from Will Adams of Keyword Ltd and Peter Townsend of Silver Link Publishing Ltd.

Philip Horton,
Lincolnshire
January 2016

Introduction

When I was growing up in the Bath of the 1950s the city boasted two major stations, Bath Spa and Bath Green Park. Living in its western suburb of Oldfield Park I found myself virtually surrounded by railways, and their sights and sounds form some of my earliest memories. From an attic window I could just see the top of trains emerging from under the bridge at the top of Brougham Hayes on their way to Bristol. From the landing window at the back of the house I watched one, sometimes two, columns of steam slowly progress behind the distant rooftops to my right until the train came briefly into view. One of our regular family Sunday walks (I didn't actually walk, I was in my pushchair!) took us to the start of the derelict Kennet & Avon Canal. This was on the River Avon below Bath Spa station and gave an impressive view of trains arriving and leaving the station. Further along the canal towpath we would reach the Sydney Gardens where there was yet another opportunity to watch trains. After walking back through the city centre we passed the front of Green Park station. Once I remember my father lifting me up to a small window in a long building near to the station, and inside I could smell the fresh straw and hear the chomping of the railway horses. A second walk took us over what is now Victoria Bridge Road to the Royal Victoria Park. The railway interest here was the cinder track that led off this road to Green Park engine shed. A siding ran from the shed next to the path and usually contained two or three silent steam engines.

Railways were also in my blood as my grandfather had been the station master at Midford on the Somerset & Dorset Joint Railway (S&D) south of Bath between 1926 and 1934. Although he died soon after I was born both my mother and grandmother were full of stories about life in the railway house there. In addition my Uncle Denis was a signalman in South London and, during his visits, was happy to talk to me about railways. He also introduced me to railway photography. It was inevitable that in the summer of 1959, at the age of 12, I should join the groups of small boys who spent their time pursuing the then popular hobby of trainspotting. As I grew older I learned that the engines on the two lines were different. At Bath Spa those mainly from the old Great Western Railway (GWR) predominated while at Green Park the engines were of London Midland & Scottish Railway (LMS) origin. The line that I could see from the back of my house was the S&D line, which ascended steeply in a 180° loop from Bath Junction on the ex-LMS's branch from Bath Green Park to Mangotsfield. I also grew up with the sounds, long since silenced, of goods wagons being shunted. The sounds came from the ex-GWR goods yard near my home, as well as from the one at Green Park.

Historically the GWR had seen the S&D and LMS trains as interlopers in its territory. By 1959, however, all the lines through Bath were part of BR's Western Region (BR(WR)). At that time the Region was rapidly implementing the Railway Modernisation Plan of 1955. Local services through Bath Spa were already worked by new diesel multiple units (DMUs), while some of the London trains, including the non-stop 'Bristolian', were hauled by one of the new 'Warship' Class diesel-hydraulic engines. The trains at Green Park, however, remained steam worked.

The rundown of the services through Green Park commenced with the announcement that its most important train, the 'Pines Express', which included coaches from Manchester, Liverpool and

MIDFORD: My grandfather is seen sitting with two of his staff outside Midford signal box during the late 1920s. The man next to him is Percy Savage, who later became a signalman at Midford and was to feature with his colleague Harry Wiltshire in Ivo Peters's many books and films of the S&D. The signal box at Midford was demolished by a runaway train in July 1935 and was subsequently rebuilt. It finally closed with the line and station on 6 March 1966. *Author's collection*

Part 1: The old order is changing, 1953-1962

Bradford to Bournemouth, would be diverted to another route from September 1962. Publication of the Beeching Report in April 1963 spelled the end of Bath Green Park altogether. By the end of 1965 the BR(WR) main line through Bath Spa was completely dieselised, and on Sunday 7 March 1966 the last train ran into Bath Green Park.

There have been a host of previous books on the S&D, many of which have concentrated on the 'Pines Express' and other through trains. Although I took few photographs of these, I did photograph some of those that ran daily through Bath Spa or into Green Park, albeit with the most basic of cameras! This book is therefore my personal record of the end of steam around Bath and of the S&D as a whole.

BATH SPA: Before the introduction of 'Warship' Class diesel-hydraulics, an unidentified ex-GWR 'Castle' Class 4-6-0 makes a fine sight as it enters Bath Spa with an express from Paddington in the summer of 1956. The coaches are still in the in BR's early 'blood and custard' livery. The line on the right goes to the old fish dock where for many years the wagons were shunted by the station horse. Note the wagon turntable in the fish dock's yard.
M. E. J. Deane collection, courtesy of Ian Bennett

STEAM THROUGH BATH SPA

By 1959 passenger train services through Bath Spa were seeing the effects of BR(WR)'s Modernisation programme. A report that some friends and I produced on a visit to the station in the autumn of 1960 describes the scene. The first two trains we saw after arriving at the station at 2.35pm were to Chippenham and Bristol Temple Meads respectively, both worked by diesel multiple units (DMUs). At 2.51pm a Paddington to Weston-super-Mare train arrived behind 'Warship' diesel-hydraulic No D801 *Vanguard*. Further DMU departures followed, interspersed with several steam-hauled trains. The first was the 11.45am from Portsmouth Harbour to Cardiff General headed by ex-GWR 'Grange' Class 4-6-0 No 6816 *Frankton Grange*.. 'Castle' Class 4-6-0 No 7019 *Fowey Castle* then arrived running slightly late with the 2.15pm from Weston-super-Mare to

Left **BROUGHAM HAYES:** The bridge at the top of Brougham Hayes was close to my home and a favourite vantage point for trainspotting. After crossing the River Avon immediately west of Bath Spa station, the main line ran straight for more than a mile. The eruption of steam from the direction of the station meant that a train was on its way. Would the engine be new to the spotter – a 'cop' – or one of the line's regulars? Another 'Castle' Class 4-6-0 approaches Brougham Hayes bridge with a Paddington to Bristol express during the summer of 1959. *Denis Horton*

Below **BROUGHAM HAYES:** An ex-GWR Class '57XX' 0-6-0 pannier tank was kept at Bath to shunt wagons in the adjacent goods yard. The shed at Bath was a sub-shed of Bristol Bath Road, and the engine returned there for any maintenance that could not be undertaken locally'; another pannier tank then took its place. Pannier tank No 9729 is seen approaching Brougham Hayes bridge while on shunting duties in the summer of 1959. The engine appears to have recently been through Swindon Works as its paintwork is clean and it sports the later BR emblem. Bristol Bath Road shed closed to steam in September 1960, while that at Bath closed altogether in February 1961. *Denis Horton*

Paddington; the first 'Castle', No 4073 *Caerphilly Castle*, had been introduced in 1923 by GWR Chief Mechanical Engineer C. B. Collett. *Fowey Castle* was one of the 38 engines built by the GWR/BR between 1946 and 1950.

The highlight of the afternoon was the arrival of ex-GWR 'King' Class 4-6-0 No 6002 *King William IV* on the up line with a train of empty coaches. The train then reversed into one of the middle two lines through the station and would later form the 4.50pm all-stations to Swindon, a running-in turn for engines recently overhauled at Swindon Works. Although a note in our report says that the train had recently been worked by BR Standard Class 5 4-6-0s, its engines often provided a surprise for local spotters, and had included the preserved ex-GWR 4-4-0 No 3440 *City of Truro*. The only freight train to

pass through the station that afternoon, behind ex-GWR pannier tank 0-6-0 No 4612, was a local pick-up goods for Bristol. Shortly after this we left on a DMU for Oldfield Park. Our report was supposed to be the first of a series, but sadly further editions failed to appear. Just five years later the official 'Farewell to Steam' special ran through the station.

Below left **OLDFIELD PARK:** The line through Bath Spa saw a steady stream of coal trains from South Wales to the South Coast via Salisbury. The train was usually hauled by an ex-GWR Class '28XX' 2-8-0 heavy freight engine or a Class '72XX' 2-8-2 tank. An early photograph taken by me in 1960 shows '28XX' 2-8-0 No 3806 passing under the bridge carrying Brook Road over the railway, and through Oldfield Park Halt. This class, designed by G. W. Churchward, first appeared in 1903, although No 3806 is one of the later versions introduced by C. B. Collett in 1938. Note the gaggle of small boys trainspotting on the opposite side of the line. *Author*

Below left **SYDNEY GARDENS:** Bath's Sydney Gardens were some distance from Oldfield Park, but sometimes formed part of my family's weekly Sunday afternoon walk. They provided splendid views of trains heading into and out of Bath Spa. My Uncle Denis visited the Gardens around 1956 to take a few photographs, and these included this view of another 'Castle' Class 4-6-0 on an express from Paddington towards Bath Spa. *Denis Horton*

Below **SYDNEY GARDENS:** Ex-GWR 'Hall' Class 4-6-0 No 6900 *Abney Hall* of Bristol Bath Road shed heads away from Bath past Sydney Gardens with a train, probably from Bristol Temple Meads to Salisbury. The coaches appear to be in BR's early 'blood and custard' livery. The railway scene through Sydney Gardens and indeed Bath as a whole is currently being transformed because of the line's electrification. *Denis Horton*

STEAM FROM BATH GREEN PARK

82F

BATH GREEN PARK ENGINE SHED

In 1959 Bath Green Park shed was part of BR(WR)'s Bristol Division and coded 82F. The shed provided engines for trains over the former S&D and LMS lines. Historically engines for the S&D line were supplied by the Midland Railway (MR) and its successor the LMS. These included several of the 'Black 5' 4-6-0s designed by William Stanier (later Sir William), which were sent to Bath in 1938. Although Green Park shed had received three new BR Standard Class 5 4-6-0s, Nos 73050 to 73052, in 1954, the last two 'Black 5s' did not return to BR(LMR) until 1958. In 1959 many of the engines at Bath still reflected their pre-nationalisation origins, the older of which were reaching the end of their careers. Three new BR Standard Class 4 4-6-0s, Nos 75071-73, arrived in 1956 to replace them and further Standard engines followed. Although BR(WR) also supplied a number of ex-GWR 0-6-0s, one of the ex-LMS engines lasted into 1966.

When I started to take a serious interest in the engines parked next to the cinder path leading to the shed they included an ancient 0-4-4 tank and two 4-4-0s, which are pictured overleaf. Unlike the engines that passed under Brougham Hayes bridge, very few of those at Green Park shed carried names. The appearance of a 'namer' was therefore something of note. In the autumn of 1959 word spread that *Lady Godiva* was on shed; this was of course not a naked lady but an unrebuilt 'Patriot' 4-6-0, No 45519, one of three based at Bristol Barrow Road shed. Then just before Christmas 1959 the spotting grapevine learned that two 'Jubilees' were at Bath. These engines were not too uncommon on the 'Pines Express', but two together was unusual. By the time I got there both engines were inside the old S&D shed and, although trainspotters were strongly discouraged, a couple of us crept inside and duly 'copped' them. The 'Jubilees' were, I believe, No 45618

BATH GREEN PARK: In 1959/60 ex-Midland Railway (MR) tank No 58086 was stored next to the cinder path at Bath. It was built in 1900 by Dubs & Co of Glasgow to the design of the MR's CME Samuel Johnson. The engines were used on passenger trains between Bath and Bristol into the 1930s. Similar engines were built for the S&D in its early years, and worked many of its main-line expresses. Four of the Midland engines survived at Highbridge shed until the early 1950s. No 58086 was the last of its class when withdrawn in August 1960. *Author*

Right **BATH GREEN PARK:** Behind No 58086 were two of the inside-cylinder 4-4-0s designed by LMS CME Henry Fowler (later Sir Henry); altogether 130 of these engines were built from 1928, including three for the S&D. The engine here is No 40698, while behind is another member of the class, thought to be either No 40696 or 40697. No 40698 was taken out of service in August 1960 but Nos 40696 and 40697 were not withdrawn until June and February 1962 respectively. One of the 7F 2-8-0s, No 53806, unique to the S&D, can be seen behind the second 4-4-0. *Denis Horton*

New Hebrides and No 45668 *Madden*, both strangers to Bath. Named 'West Country' 'Pacifics' from Bournemouth shed also appeared regularly on relief trains at Bank Holidays and on summer Saturdays. On 24 December 1959 'West Country' Class No 34028 *Eddystone* famously arrived at Bath with the 'Pines Express' assisted by Green Park's 0-6-0 'Jinty' tank No 47496, which had been attached at Radstock.

⊙ **82F** ⊙

An even more unusual 'namer' to appear on 31 May 1960 was ex-LNER Class 'B1' 4-6-0 No 61027 *Mandoqua* (named after a small antelope or 'dik-dik'). I was lucky enough to see it pass Westerleigh the next day with the up 'Pines Express'. 1961 was the summer of the 'Royal Scots' at Bath. One afternoon I was amazed to see No 46100 *Royal Scot* itself parked at the shed end of the cinder track. Several other 'Scots' appeared that year, but unfortunately I managed to lose my notebook for that period. I do, however, remember one Sunday finding No 46106 *Gordon Highlander* parked alongside the old Midland shed. Unlike all the other 'Royal Scots', *Gordon Highlander* was fitted with Standard BR smoke deflectors. On an earlier Sunday visit a much smaller engine was parked on the same bit of line. This was No 47190, the last of two 0-4-0 'Sentinel' engines built in 1929. Their small size allowed them to pass under a low bridge when shunting one of the colliery sidings at Radstock. The engine had been withdrawn in August 1959 and was on its way to be broken up. The only 'Royal Scot' I recorded during 1962 was No 46157 *The Royal Artilleryman*.

Below right **BATH GREEN PARK:** The next two views of engines show them in steam, on the siding next to the access track into Green Park shed. Here No 44558 awaits its next call of duty during 1962. Fowler built more than 750 of these 0-6-0s for the MR and LMS from 1911, including five for the S&D (latterly Nos 44557 to 44561). No 44558 was built by Armstrong Whitworth & Co of Newcastle in 1922. Although essentially goods engines, they were regularly used on passenger trains on the S&D, including piloting the summer specials. All five remained on the line into the 1960s. No 44558 was withdrawn in December 1964, but No 44560 lasted until September 1965. *Author*

INDUSTRIAL STEAM IN BATH

BATH GREEN PARK: During the winter of 1961 BR(WR) carried out clearance trials for ex-GWR Class '28XX' 2-8-0s between Mangotsfield and Bath Green Park. A number of the class subsequently worked into the city with pigeon specials from the Midlands. One of the Class, No 2859 of Pontypool Road shed, is pictured on 4 August 1962 after arrival with one of the trains. At the time racing pigeons were taken by special train to a distant destination and released to return home. No 2859 was built in 1918 and was withdrawn in December 1964. After a spell at Barry scrapyard it was purchased for preservation, but so far remains unrestored at Llangollen. *Author*

BATH GASWORKS: Bath gasworks' two industrial tank engines were easy to miss. They could sometimes be glimpsed from a passing train or through the gasworks entrance on what is now Windsor Bridge Road. The two 0-4-0 saddle tanks, which were both built in Bristol, are pictured outside their engine shed in 1960. In the foreground is a Peckett of 1912 (works No 1267), while behind is an Avonside of 1928 (works No 1978). Stothert & Pitt's extensive factory, where it built dockyard cranes, lay between the gasworks and Green Park shed and, although it had a railway system, road tractors were used to marshal the bogie bolster wagons on which its products were despatched. These reached the ex-Midland main line by way of a line through Green Park's shed yard. *M. E. J. Deane collection, courtesy of Ian Bennett*

THE FORMER SOMERSET & DORSET LINE TO TEMPLECOMBE

The multitude of published photos of the summer Saturday trains that ran between Bournemouth and the towns of the industrial north and Midlands via Bath tend to give the impression that the S&D was a busy main line. While this was true of summer Saturdays, things were fairly quiet for the rest of the year. On weekdays in September 1956 just 11 passenger trains climbed Devonshire Bank out of Bath. Five of these ran to Bournemouth West, one of which, the 'Pines Express', came from Manchester while the other four were through trains from Bristol Temple Meads. All five had reversed at Green Park station. Five more trains terminated at Templecombe, while the 6.05pm from Bath was for Binegar.

'The 'Pines Express' was the fastest train of the day between Bath and Bournemouth, taking 2hr 27min for the 72½ miles. The slowest, at 3hr 49min, was the 6.55am from Bath, although this included a 24-minute wait at Templecombe. In 1956 the through trains were hauled by one of the remaining 'Black 5s' or one of the new Standard Class 5s. The 'Pines Express' would typically leave Bath behind one of the Class 5 engines and an ex-S&D or LMS 4-4-0. The latter also shared the work on the local trains with ex-S&D or LMS 0-6-0s, although the newly acquired Standard Class 4 engines were starting to replace them. From 1959 ex-GWR 0-6-0s from Templecombe shed also began to appear

Left **BATH GREEN PARK:** Passenger trains over the S&D line, including the 'Pines Express', were hauled by 2P 4-4-0s until replaced by LMS 'Black 5' 4-6-0s from 2 May 1938. Five of these remained at Bath, on loan from BR(LMR), after the Western Region takeover, and the last two were not handed back until 1958. 'Black 5s' still regularly worked the 'Pines Express' north of Bath until September 1961, but their duties on the S&D were progressively taken over by new Standard Class 5 4-6-0s. One of Bath's 'Black 5s', No 44826, is seen here on empty carriage stock on one of Bath Green Park's central roads in 1953. At the time Green Park shed was under BR(SR) control and coded 73G. *Denis Horton*

Above **RINGWOOD ROAD:** The 3.20pm from Bath Green Park to Templecombe was regularly hauled by one of the 2P 4-4-0s, a duty they shared with their contemporaries, the 4F 0-6-0s. At the end of the summer of 1961 the 4-4-0s were stored or withdrawn, but early in 1962 No 40563 of Templecombe shed was used on the train. I photographed it from the back lane that ran behind Ringwood Road, shortly after the train, comprising ex-SR coach set No 390, had crossed the BR(WR) main line. An earlier photograph of No 40563 climbing out of Bath appears on the front cover of this book. No 40563 was one of the last of the 4-4-0s to be withdrawn, in May 1962. *Author*

MIDFORD: Ex-S&D and LMS 4F 0-6-0 goods engines were extensively used on passenger trains on the S&D, and one is seen leaving Midford in the summer of 1956. The three-coach set of Maunsell vehicles is still in BR's early 'blood and custard' livery.

The Southern Railway was responsible for supplying the coaching stock for S&D trains and in 1926 its CME, R. E. L. Maunsell, built a number of three-coach sets for use in the West Country. These included Nos 390 to 399, which were used on the S&D to replace earlier ex-London & South Western stock. They were all withdrawn by the end of 1961 to be replaced on the S&D by more modern ex-GWR, LMS and SR 'Bulleid' coaches. *M. E. J. Deane collection, courtesy of Ian Bennett*

on these duties. The 4-4-0s lasted as pilot engines on the 'Pines' and the summer expresses until the end of the summer of 1961, after which they were put into store. Despite the increasing numbers of 'Standards', ex-S&D, LMS or GWR 0-6-0s continued to work the local trains. The 6.05pm to Binegar was usually worked by one of Green Park's Ivatt Class 2 or Standard Class 3 2-6-2 tanks.

Goods traffic was worked by the 11 unique S&D 7F 2-8-0s or by ex-S&D or LMS 0-6-0s, then LMS 8F 2-8-0s started to replace the 7Fs from October 1961. Until the 1960s much freight between Bath and Templecombe was destined for Devon and Cornwall. Prior to nationalisation the LMS and SR (joint operators of the S&D) had routed this over the S&D via Templecombe to avoid paying tolls to the GWR. This clearly made no sense when the direct GWR route via Taunton was now available. BR(WR) therefore started to divert freight away from the S&D. Sadly, virtually all of this traffic was subsequently lost to the railways. At the time much freight was being transferred to road transport, but the inept way that BR introduced changes to its freight services also contributed to its loss.

BATH GREEN PARK: The 11 unique S&D 7F 2-8-0 goods engines were popular for use on enthusiasts' excursions. Here No 53804 waits at Bath Green Park to have its headboard fitted before working a Stephenson Locomotive Society (SLS) special over the S&D on Sunday 11 September 1960. No 53804 was one of the first six engines built by the Midland Railway specifically for the S&D in 1914 to the design of Henry Fowler, and all were allocated to Green Park shed. No 53804 was one of the last two of the original engines to be withdrawn in February 1962. Five further engines were provided in 1923, the last of which, No 53807, was not withdrawn until October 1964. *M. E. J. Deane collection, courtesy of Ian Bennett*

Below: **MIDFORD:** The Class 2P/Standard Class 5 combination is pictured again in June 1961 as No 40569 and a Class 5 head the 'Pines Express' away from Midford. No 40569 will be detached at Evercreech Junction to return light engine to its shed at Templecombe. The 2P was withdrawn in November 1961. *M. E. J. Deane collection, courtesy of Ian Bennett*

**Ex-S&D/LMS
2P 4-4-0s and Standard Class 5 4-6-0s
on the 'Pines Express' in 1961**

Above: **BATH:** In 1954 Bath Green Park shed received three new Standard Class 5 4-6-0s. 'The Pines Express' was then usually made up of one of these engines and twelve ex-LMS coaches. An ex-LMS or S&D 2P 4-4-0 assisted the train out of Bath and over the Mendip Hills as far as Evercreech Junction. In this view of 'The Pines Express' climbing out of Bath in April 1961, the 2P is no. 40634 of Templecombe shed, one of three engines built specifically for the S&D in 1930. After September 1961 the 4-4-0s were largely replaced by Standard Class 4 4-6-0s although no.40563 saw use on the 3.20pm to Templecombe into 1962 as pictured earlier in the book. Both Nos. 40634 and 40563 were among the last of their class to be withdrawn in May 1962. *M. E. J. Deane collection, courtesy of Ian Bennett*

THE FORMER MIDLAND LINE TO MANGOTSFIELD

In September 1956 10 trains left Green Park each weekday for Bristol Temple Meads via Mangotsfield, three of which were through trains from Bournemouth West. There were also two trains on Sundays, which were extended to Bournemouth during the summer. These last ran in the summer of 1961. The 15-mile journey to Bristol took some 40 minutes compared with just 16 minutes for the 11¼ miles from Bath Spa. However, I often used these trains to travel to Bristol as they passed the ex-LMS shed at Barrow Road, where one or two interesting engines were likely to be spotted. The fare was the same for both routes. In 1950 ex-LMS Class 2P 0-4-4 tanks, built by William Stanier from 1932, were still used on the local trains to Bristol. These were soon replaced by H. G. Ivatt's Class 2 2-6-2 tanks, followed later by BR Standard Class 3 2-6-2 tank engines. The 'Pines Express' to Manchester also took this route out of Bath, but just before Mangotsfield station it turned right at Mangotsfield South Junction to join the Bristol to Birmingham New Street line at Mangotsfield North Junction. The train was normally worked by a 'Black 5' 4-6-0 but in the summer of 1960/61 it could be

Above **BATH:** Besides working heavy goods trains on the S&D line, the 7F 2-8-0s were also used on trains to and from the north. Here No 53808 arrives in Bath tender first with a goods train from Westerleigh on 27 June 1962. This was one of the second batch of five engines that were built for the line in 1925 by Robert Stephenson & Co of Newcastle. The engine is unusually clean and may have recently received attention at Derby Works. *Author*

headed by anything from a 'Royal Scot' to a 'B1'. 'Peak ' Class diesel-electrics took over from 10 September 1961.

Goods traffic from the north was usually hauled by an ex-LMS 4F 0-6-0, 8F 2-8-0 or Standard Class 5 engines. The ex-S&D's 7F 2-8-0s were also used, especially on trains to and from Westerleigh, the LMS's marshalling yard to the north of Bristol, or to Bristol East Depot.

Above **BATH GREEN PARK:** Ivatt Class 2 2-6-2 tank No 41296, one of the class that replaced the 0-4-4 tanks on trains between Green Park and Bristol from 1950, is pictured on the main line next to Green Park shed on 18 August 1962. It had just reversed out of the station after working in with a train from Bristol Temple Meads. At the time these Ivatt engines were being replaced by Standard Class 3 2-6-2 tanks, and were later concentrated at Templecombe shed, where they worked local trains including those on the branch line to Highbridge. No 41296 was transferred there in July 1965 and was one of the last S&D-based engines to be withdrawn, in March 1966. *Author*

THE LAST YEAR OF THE 'PINES EXPRESS' AND SUMMER SATURDAY TRAINS, 1962

Summer Saturdays saw many holiday trains routed over the ex-S&D line. Traditionally these were double-headed on the steep gradient out of Bath and over Masbury summit in the Mendip Hills. The introduction of 9F 2-10-0s from the summer of 1960 reduced the need for this, but double-heading was still quite common. Despite the presence of the powerful 2-10-0s, the S&D 7F 2-8-0s were also still at work in the summer of 1962. All through trains, including the 'Pines', were diverted away from the S&D line from 10 September 1962.

Above left **DEVONSHIRE BANK:** A train often headed by one of the ex-S&D 7F 2-8-0s in the summer of 1962 was the 7.00am Saturdays-only (SO) from Cleethorpes to Sidmouth and Exmouth. On Saturday 18 August the train was photographed climbing Devonshire Bank behind No 53810 assisted by Standard Class 4 4-6-0 No 75009. The train will join the BR(SR) Waterloo to Exeter main line at Templecombe, where the 2-8-0 wouldl be replaced by a Southern engine. The up train to Cleethorpes had arrived earlier at Green Park behind 7F No 53808. The engines on the down train on 4 August had been ex-S&D 0-6-0 No 44559, again assisted by a Standard Class 4 4-6-0. *Charles Huff, author's collection*

Above centre **DEVONSHIRE BANK:** This is the unusual sight of two Standard Class 5 4-6-0s, the first of which is Green Park's No 73051, starting their descent into Bath with another of the Summer Saturday trains from Bournemouth West to the Midlands on 18 August 1962. *Charles Huff, author's collection*

Above **DEVONSHIRE BANK:** No 92233 was one of the four powerful 9F 2-10-0s allocated to Bath Green Park shed in July 1962, and needs no assistance as it hauls the 7.45am (SO) Bradford to Bournemouth West train out of Bath on 18 August 1962. No 92233 had earlier worked into Bath with the 8.40am (SO) from Bournemouth West to Derby. *Charles Huff, author's collection*

Below **BATH GREEN PARK:** During the summer of 1962 the 'Pines Express' was usually hauled out of Bath by a Standard Class 4 4-6-0 and 9F 2-10-0. However, on Wednesday 15 August the engines used were Standard Class 4 2-6-0 No 76009 of Eastleigh shed and Green Park's Standard Class 5 No 73054. No 76009 is carrying the 'Pines Express' headboard, which only appeared for the last few weeks of the train's association with the S&D. *Author*

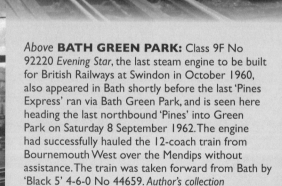

Above **BATH GREEN PARK:** Class 9F No 92220 *Evening Star*, the last steam engine to be built for British Railways at Swindon in October 1960, also appeared in Bath shortly before the last 'Pines Express' ran via Bath Green Park, and is seen here heading the last northbound 'Pines' into Green Park on Saturday 8 September 1962. The engine had successfully hauled the 12-coach train from Bournemouth West over the Mendips without assistance. The train was taken forward from Bath by 'Black 5' 4-6-0 No 44659. *Author's collection*

STEAM THROUGH BATH SPA

By 1963 virtually all passenger trains calling at Bath Spa had been diesel-worked for at least a year, and the appearance of a steam engine usually meant that one of the new diesels had failed. This may explain my last sighting of a 'Castle' on a timetabled express from Paddington on Saturday 20 July 1963. The engine was No 7029 *Clun Castle*, which I saw leaving Chippenham on time with the 9.45am to Weston-super-Mare. *Clun Castle* was to work BR's 'Farewell to Steam' special on 27 November 1965 (see page 27). The engine was withdrawn from Gloucester Horton Road shed in December 1965 and is now preserved at the Birmingham Railway Museum, Tyseley.

My last sight of a steam engine on a train from Paddington occurred in the spring of 1964. I was returning by bus to Oldfield Park when I spotted the once familiar plume of steam over Bath Spa. I just had time to get off the bus and rush to Brougham Hayes bridge to see the last working 'County' Class 4-6-0, No 1011 *County of Chester*, pass underneath. The train was the 1.45pm from Paddington to Weston-super-Mare, and was running almost an hour late. It was also the only London train to call at Oldfield Park. No 1011 was withdrawn in November 1964 and I photographed it later at Cashmore's scrapyard in Newport.

A handful of regular passenger trains through Bath Spa did, however, remain steam-hauled into 1964, and two that I was aware of both called at Oldfield Park. The crisp exhaust of their ex-GWR engines could clearly be heard from the house as they accelerated their trains towards Bath Spa. The first was the early-morning 6.38am (Saturdays excepted) from Avonmouth Dock to Westbury via Bristol (Stapleton Road), while in the early evening the 7.00pm from Bristol Temple Meads also ran to Westbury; this train disappeared at the start of the summer timetable in June 1964, but the Avonmouth train survived until the end of the summer.

The summer of 1964 saw the appearance of a new steam-hauled passenger train through Bath Spa. This was the 6.10pm (Sundays only) from Weston-super-Mare to Swindon, which was scheduled to run until 6 September, and I managed to photograph it several times before the end of the summer. All these trains were usually hauled by one of the 'Halls' allocated to Bristol St Philip's Marsh shed. This closed in June 1964 when its remaining steam engines were transferred to the former LMS shed at Barrow Road. A handful of Summer Saturday trains were also steam-hauled in 1964 including the 9.13am from Bournemouth Central to Swansea High Street.

During 1965 the number of steam-hauled goods trains through Bath was boosted by special workings from BR(SR). These trains were made up of condemned steam engines from the BR's Southern Region en route to scrapyards in South Wales. On

TWERTON: One of the last steam-hauled trains through Bath Spa was the 7.00pm from Bristol Temple Meads to Westbury, pictured here heading for Twerton Tunnel behind ex-GWR 'Hall' Class 4-6-0 No 6908 *Downham Hall* in April 1964. The train was withdrawn from Monday 15 June, although the 6.38am (Saturdays excepted) from Avonmouth Dock to Westbury continued to run into the summer. *Author*

15 October 1965 I saw 'West Country' 'Pacific' No 34032 *Camelford* waiting in the down goods loop at Bathampton with Standard Class 4 2-6-4 tanks Nos 80088, 80066, 80084 and 80081 in tow. Its destination was not Barry Docks, as none of the tanks was later preserved. While at Bathampton, 'Hall' Class No 4920 *Dumbleton Hall*, running without name or number plates, passed light engine towards Swindon. This was one of the last of BR(WR)'s 'Halls'

to be withdrawn in December 1965. It did go to Barry scrapyard, but is now preserved at the South Devon Railway.

Even after the 'Farewell to Steam' special on 27 November 1965, a handful of goods trains remained steam-worked including the 10.15pm goods from Bristol East Depot to Banbury. With the exception of those on the S&D line at Bath, BR(WR) withdrew the last of its steam engines at the end of December 1965.

Left **BATHAMPTON:** On Sunday 12 July 1964 the train from Weston-super-Mare was hauled by BR-built 'Modified Hall' 4-6-0 No 7917 *North Aston Hall*, and I managed to photograph it passing Bathampton station. Between Weston-super-Mare and Bristol Temple Meads the train called only at Parson Street and Bedminster. It then called at Keynsham & Somerdale, Oldfield Park, Bath Spa, Chippenham and Swindon. *Author*

Below **OLDFIELD PARK:** The 6.10pm (Sundays only) from Weston-super-Mare to Swindon appeared at the start of the summer timetable in June 1964 and ran until 6 September, being steam-worked throughout that period. On Sunday 28 June ex-GWR 'Hall' Class 4-6-0 No 6900 *Abney Hall* (seen earlier in the book passing Sydney Gardens) is seen leaving Oldfield Park station with the train. *Author*

Below **BATH SPA:** On the train's penultimate Sunday, 30 August, I travelled on it between Oldfield Park and Chippenham. It was hauled by BR-built 'Castle' Class 4-6-0 No 7024 *Powis Castle*, and is pictured at Bath Spa. It will be noted that semaphore signals still controlled train movements through the station. These were operated from the signal box situated on the roof of the down platform, just visible above the tender of No 7024. Although the 'Castle' lacked a front number plate and was in a filthy condition, it produced an exhilarating run through Box Tunnel to Chippenham. *Powis Castle* came from the ex-GWR shed at Oxley, Wolverhampton, by then part of BR(LMR), and was withdrawn in February 1965. *Author*

Left **OLDFIELD PARK:** On 22 August Standard Class 5 4-6-0 No 73082 *Camelot* passes under the S&D line at Oldfield Park with what is thought to be the 9.13am Saturdays-only train from Bournemouth Central to Swansea High Street (the engine is seen again later at Green Park shed on page 29). It was withdrawn from Guildford shed in June 1966 and, after a spell in Barry scrapyard, was purchased for preservation; it is now active on the heritage Bluebell Railway in East Sussex. *Author*

Above **OLDFIELD PARK:** Steam still appeared on the many goods trains that ran through Bath Spa, including the coal trains from South Wales to Portsmouth. Standard Class 9F 2-10-0 No 92248 approaches Oldfield Park station with one of the trains during September 1964. Like the rest of the class, this 9F had a short working life; built at Crewe in December 1958, it was withdrawn from Cardiff East Dock shed in June 1965. *Author*

Left **OLDFIELD PARK:** A 'Hymek' diesel-hydraulic in trouble: ex-GWR 0-6-0 pannier tank No 9790 passes under Brougham Hayes bridge and approaches Oldfield Park station with a failed 'Hymek' on 25 May 1965. Diesel failures were relatively common at the time. *Author*

BATH SPA: The trains of withdrawn engines that ran through Bath Spa to scrapyards in South Wales continued after the end of steam on BR(WR). On several occasions the engines 'ran hot' and had to be detached at Bath. Here 'Bulleid' 'Q1' Class 0-6-0 No 33020, withdrawn in January 1966, stands in the former goods yard at Bath on 27 April 1966. I photographed it again at Cashmore's scrapyard in Newport. *Author*

STEAM SPECIALS THROUGH BATH 1964-65

BATH JUNCTION: The Home Counties Railway Society's 'Somerset & Dorset' rail tour ran on Sunday 7 June 1964. The tour started at Waterloo, ran over the S&D line from Bournemouth Central to Evercreech Junction, then visited Highbridge before setting off again from Evercreech Junction for Bath. The organisers had hoped to use two of the line's 7F 2-8-0s, but in the event only 7F No 53807 was available. Ex-S&D 4F 0-6-0s No 44558 was therefore used as the second engine instead. I was ill with a mystery virus at the time, but saw the train descending Devonshire Bank from my landing window. Fortunately M. E. J. Deane was at Bath Junction to record Nos 53807 and 44558 coming off the S&D line with the train. *M. E. J. Deane collection, courtesy of Ian Bennett*

BATH JUNCTION: The rail tour was hauled from Green Park to Gloucester Eastgate by BR-built 'Castle' Class 4-6-0 No 7023 *Penrice Castle*. The train is seen approaching Bath Junction again en route for Gloucester, from where it ran to Paddington behind sister engine No 7025 *Sudeley Castle*. This is thought to be the only appearance of a 'Castle' at Bath Green Park. *M. E. J. Deane collection, courtesy of Ian Bennett*

Left **OLDFIELD PARK:** On 30 September 1964 the Great Western Society ran a 'Bolliver's Travels' special, which travelled over several ex-GWR branch lines, including that to Calne, using auto-fitted 0-4-2 tank No 1444 and two push-pull coaches. Although of ancient appearance, No 1444 was built only in 1935. The train is seen approaching Oldfield Park en route for Bristol Temple Meads. At the time a number of the class were still active on BR(WR), including the Gloucester Central to Chalford train service. This was withdrawn from Monday 2 November, together with its engines, which included No 1444. *Author*

Above **TWERTON TUNNEL:** The following year, on Sunday 4 April 1965, both Mr Deane and I were able to record the passage of the 'Wessex Downsman Rail Tour' organised by the Locomotive Club of Great Britain (LCGB). The train ran from Waterloo to Reading General behind SR Class 'S15' 4-6-0 No 30837. From Reading it was taken forward by one of the declining number of ex-GWR 'Hall' Class 4-6-0s, and here we see 'Modified Hall' No 6963 *Throwley Hall* (running without nameplates) leaving Twerton Tunnel. The train had travelled via Devizes and Bradford-on-Avon and was running some 50 minutes late. *Author*

Left **BITTON:** From Bristol Temple Meads the 'Wessex Downsman' travelled to Mangotsfield behind 'Hymek' diesel-hydraulic No D7007 and ex-LMS 4F 0-6-0 No 44466. The diesel was detached at Mangotsfield, and No 44466 is seen later approaching Bitton, bound for Bath Green Park. *M. E. J. Deane collection, courtesy of Ian Bennett*

DEVONSHIRE BANK: Now running more than an hour late, 8F 2-8-0 No 48309 struggles up the 1 in 50 of Devonshire Bank at walking pace with the ten-coach train. The 8F had been allocated to Bath Green Park shed in August 1964. *Author*

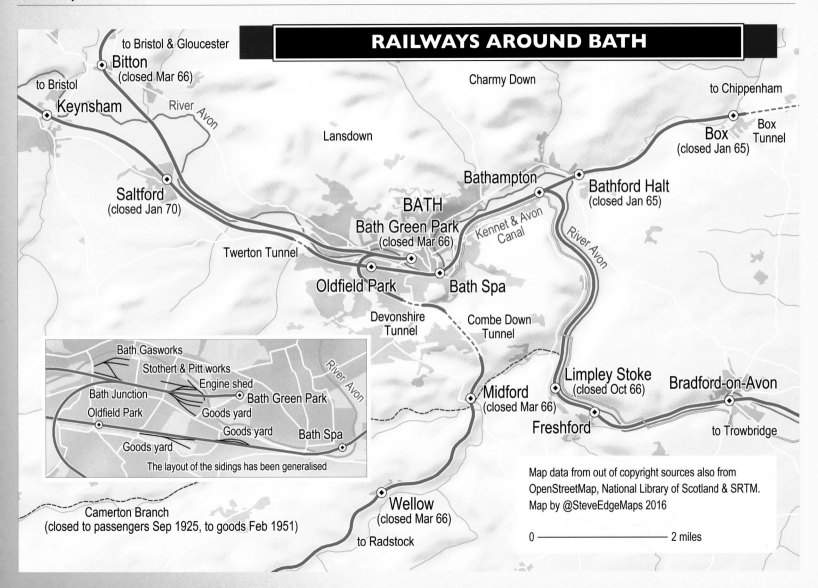

RAILWAYS AROUND BATH

to Bristol & Gloucester

Bitton
(closed Mar 66)

Charmy Down

to Chippenham

to Bristol

Keynsham

River Avon

Lansdown

Box
(closed Jan 65)

Box Tunnel

Saltford
(closed Jan 70)

Bathampton

Bathford Halt
(closed Jan 65)

BATH

Bath Green Park
(closed Mar 66)

Kennet & Avon Canal

River Avon

Twerton Tunnel

Oldfield Park

Bath Spa

Devonshire Tunnel

Combe Down Tunnel

River Avon

Bath Gasworks

Stothert & Pitt works

Engine shed

Bath Junction

Bath Green Park

Oldfield Park

Goods yard

Goods yard

Bath Spa

Goods yard

The layout of the sidings has been generalised

Limpley Stoke
(closed Oct 66)

Bradford-on-Avon

Midford
(closed Mar 66)

Freshford

to Trowbridge

Map data from out of copyright sources also from OpenStreetMap, National Library of Scotland & SRTM.
Map by @SteveEdgeMaps 2016

Camerton Branch
(closed to passengers Sep 1925, to goods Feb 1951)

Wellow
(closed Mar 66)

to Radstock

0 ———————— 2 miles

DEVONSHIRE BANK: No 48309 is seen making better progress on the slightly gentler gradient towards Devonshire Tunnel. The engine was one of only two of its class with steam heating equipment, which had been fitted when, with 8F No 48707, it had hauled the Royal Train over part of the Central Wales line on 6 August 1955. *M. E. J. Deane collection, courtesy of Ian Bennett*

BATH SPA: On 27 November 1965 BR(WR) ran its own 'Farewell to Steam' rail tour, hauled by the last BR-owned 'Castle' Class 4-6-0, No 7029 *Clun Castle*. It is seen approaching Bath Spa on its run from Paddington to Gloucester Eastgate via Mangotsfield. Here 'Western' Class diesel-hydraulic No 1006 *Western Stalwart* took the train forward to Cheltenham Malvern Road. After its return to Gloucester Central *Clun Castle* took over again for the run back to Swindon. the tour was then diesel-hauled back to Paddington. *Clun Castle* was withdrawn from Gloucester Horton Road shed in December 1965 and is now preserved at the Birmingham Railway Museum, Tyseley. *Author*

82F

BATH GREEN PARK ENGINE SHED

After the loss of the 'Pines Express', the engines at Green Park shed continued to work the remaining goods and passenger trains, and the replacement of older examples by Standard classes continued. During 1963 Bournemouth shed received a number of Standard Class 4 2-6-4 tanks, which had been replaced by dieselisation and electrification elsewhere on BR. The number seen on the S&D steadily increased and in September 1964 three, Nos 80043/59/67, were allocated to Templecombe shed, with more to follow. The replacement of the former S&D 2-8-0s by Stanier 8F 2-8-0s and the S&D and LMS 0-6-0s by BR Standard engines was virtually complete by the end of 1964. The Standard engines included some of the S&D stalwarts, including Class 5s Nos 73051 and 73052 together with Class 4s Nos 75072 and 75073. No 73051 sometimes found itself well away from the S&D line. On 15 May 1965 it was to be seen heading away from Oxford with the Newcastle to Bournemouth through train, while some three years earlier, on Sunday 26 August 1962, I came across it on Stockport shed,

having clearly been called upon to work one of the Summer Saturday trains from Green Park to the North West. It would have been a rare 'cop' for local trainspotters. Although Green Park shed remained part of BR(WR)'s Bristol Division, coded 82F, Templecombe shed was transferred to its Exeter Division and recoded 83G (from 82G) in October 1963.

Named engines were a rarity at Green Park, although No 92220 *Evening Star* returned there for a spell in the summer of 1963. 'West Country' 'Pacifics' also continued to appear occasionally on trains from Bournemouth and on special workings. These included No 34047 *Callington*, which worked the 4.20pm Bristol Temple Meads to Bournemouth West on Monday 1 February. This was rather ironic

BATH GREEN PARK SHED: From the end of 1960 a number of ex-GWR Class '2251' 0-6-0s were allocated to Templecombe shed, where they worked the Highbridge branch and local passenger trains to Bath. A visit to Green Park shed in the spring of 1964 found three withdrawn members of the class en route to a scrapyard. One of them was class pioneer No 2251, introduced in 1930 by C. B. Collett. It was allocated to Templecombe in November 1963 but was withdrawn the following month. The last of its class to be allocated to Templecombe in May 1965, No 3205, was withdrawn the same month, but was subsequently preserved and is still active on the heritage South Devon Railway at Buckfastleigh. *Author*

Below **BATH GREEN PARK SHED:** An unusual visitor to Green Park shed on Sunday 29 March 1964 was Standard Class 5 4-6-0 No 73082 *Camelot*, a name formerly carried by a Southern Railway 'King Arthur' Class 4-6-0. *Camelot* was from Nine Elms shed in London and its presence was a reminder that in the summers of 1959, 1960 and 1961 its shed-mate, No 73087 *Linette*, was sent to Green Park to help work the Saturday holiday trains. Standing next to No 73082 in the old wooden S&D shed is ex-S&D 7F 2-8-0 No 53807, the last working member of the class, which was finally withdrawn that October. *Author*

Above **BATH GREEN PARK SHED:** Despite the influx of ex-GWR and BR Standard engines Fowler's 4F 0-6-0s remained active into 1964. Ex-LMS No 44146 stands outside the old Midland shed at Bath Green Park on Sunday 29 March 1964. Built at Derby in 1925, it was withdrawn in November 1964. The last member of the class I saw on the 3.20pm from Green Park to Templecombe was the now preserved No 44422 on 20 July 1964; this engine was withdrawn in June 1965, while the last of those built for the S&D, No 44560, survived until September 1965. *Author*

as the previous Saturday I had travelled to Tilehurst near Reading to photograph Sir Winston Churchill's funeral train. While waiting, the down 'Pines Express' appeared on its new route via Oxford, headed by *Callington*! As pictured on page 37, in the spring of 1965 No 34046 *Braunton*, was used on the 4.21pm to Bournemouth on several occasions. On Saturday

I May it was at Green Park with BR 'Britannia' 'Pacific' No 70034 *Thomas Hardy*. Although a handful of other 'Britannias' also visited Bath, I always missed them. The last record I can find of a 'West Country' 'Pacific' on a service train at Bath Green Park is No 34044 *Woolacombe* on 6 November 1965.

During the winter of 1964/65 two ex-GWR Class '94XX' 0-6-0 pannier tanks, Nos 8436 and 8486, were allocated to Green Park to haul the loaded coal wagons that had arrived from Radstock on to Portishead Power Station. They were the only examples to be shedded there, but both were withdrawn in June 1965. The class, which had been introduced by CME F. W. Hawksworth as recently as 1947, was then extinct on BR, although two examples, Nos 9400 and 9466, are preserved.

Below and below right **BATH GREEN PARK GOODS YARD:** Despite the influx of ex-GWR pannier tanks, ex-LMS 'Jinty' 0-6-0 tanks continued to share the shunting and banking duties at Green Park until closure. Seven 'Jinties' were built specifically for the S&D by the LMS in 1929, but all but one, No 47316, withdrawn in October 1962, later moved away from the line. The first picture shows 'Jinty' tank No 47544 shunting the goods yard at Bath on 23 August 1965; it had arrived from Bristol Barrow Road in March 1962 and was not withdrawn until December 1965.

Ex-GWR '57XX' Class pannier tank No 8745 is seen at the same location on 30 December 1963; this had come to Bath that November and was withdrawn in August 1965. This location at the throat of the goods yard was reached through a gate in a wall on Victoria Bridge Street, just before the railway overbridge. A sign on the gate read 'British Transport Commission, Trespassers will be Prosecuted' but this failed to intimidate the local spotters. One of the two Yard Inspectors was tolerant of our presence – the appearance of the other led to a hurried exit! Note the ex-MR lower-quadrant shunting signal. *Both author*

Left **BATH GREEN PARK SHED:** No 53807 was not the only ex-S&D 2-8-0 at Green Park on 29 March 1964. Standing next to the old stone-built MR shed was sister engine No 53808, withdrawn earlier that month. Unlike No 53807, No 53808 was sent to Barry scrapyard and was purchased for preservation by the Somerset & Dorset Railway Trust and is now active on the West Somerset Railway. Like No 53807 it is one of the five later engines built by Robert Stephenson & Co at Newcastle in 1925. When first built these carried larger boilers, which were replaced by standard Derby ones in BR days. Although No 53808 (S&D No 88) looked splendid when running in its S&D Prussian Blue livery, this was historically incorrect. No 53809 also went to Barry and is now preserved at the heritage Midland Railway Centre at Butterley near Derby. *Author*

THE FORMER SOMERSET & DORSET LINE TO TEMPLECOMBE

Apart from the loss of the 'Pines Express', the timetable for the S&D line from 10 September 1962 remained the same. The 3.20pm stopping train from Green Park to Templecombe continued to run even though its main purpose had been to provide a connection off the 'Pines' for all stations to Evercreech Junction.

The effects of the heavy snowfall over the Mendips during the severe winter of 1962/63 are well illustrated in Ivo Peters's books on the S&D. Early in January I remember waiting at Green Park station to catch the 10.10am to Bristol Temple Meads. No trains had yet arrived off the S&D line when two 4F 0-6-0s appeared hauling a long rake of coaches, which I presume had come from Templecombe; doors opened along the length of the train to disgorge dozens of commuters. The S&D line trains were certainly welcomed in severe weather, but at other times most of the commuters would have probably used their cars. When I travelled from Evercreech Junction to Bath on 8 March 1963 patches of snow were still lying in the fields around Masbury.

The number of unusual engines at Bath decreased significantly although, as mentioned above, the appearance of a 'West Country' 'Pacific' occasionally relieved the monotony, as did the unexpected return of *Evening Star* in the summer of 1963. By the end of 1964 Class 8Fs dominated the remaining goods trains. The local goods yards had, however, closed during 1963, while the remaining through goods traffic was diverted to other routes from September 1964. Only a single goods to Evercreech Junction and the coal trains from Radstock remained.

Above and overleaf **BATH GREEN PARK:** Although the 'Pines Express' and other holiday trains no longer ran via the S&D line, 9F 2-10-0 No 92220 *Evening Star* was again allocated to Green Park shed in August 1963, together with No 92224, where it was used on the remaining service trains between Bath and Bournemouth West. One of these trains, thought to be the 3.35pm from Bristol Temple Meads and comprised of a Bulleid three-coach set and a luggage van, is seen entering Green Park terminus behind Standard Class 3 2-6-2 tank No 82041. After backing onto the train, *Evening Star* is then seen leaving for the run over the Mendips to Bournemouth West. *Evening Star* was withdrawn from Cardiff East Dock for preservation in March 1965. Two further 9Fs reappeared briefly at Bath in the summer of 1964. *Both M. E. J. Deane collection, courtesy of Ian Bennett*

Below **BATH GREEN PARK:** A late working of an ex-LMS 4F 0-6-0 was of No 44422 on the 3.20pm to Templecombe, seen here leaving Bath on 20 July 1964. On the left is an ex-LMS Stanier 8F 2-8-0, which has arrived tender-first with a freight off the ex-S&D line. No 44422 was built in 1927 and withdrawn in June 1965. After spending 12 years in Woodham's scrapyard in Barry, it was restored to working order and has since appeared on a number of heritage railways. *Author*

Above **BATH GREEN PARK:** Green Park's Standard Class 5 4-6-0 No 73049 backs onto the 9.03am from Bristol Temple Meads to Bournemouth West. The green-liveried Class 5 was among the first of its class to be allocated to Green Park, and later spent time at Shrewsbury and Bristol Barrow Road before returning in June 1962. In September 1964 it left Bath again for Oxford, where it was withdrawn in March 1965. *Author*

Opposite **DEVONSHIRE BANK:** A suitable place to photograph trains climbing out of Bath towards Devonshire Tunnel was the site of the former Victoria Brickworks, which were once served by a siding off the S&D line. By 1964 the usual motive power for the 3.20pm from Green Park to Templecombe was a Standard Class 4 4-6-0. On 12 August No 75008 is pictured with the train climbing past the former brickworks; the first coach appears to be of LMS origin. No 75008 had been allocated to Templecombe shed in July but

moved to Exmouth Junction at the end of August. It was withdrawn from Worcester shed in December 1965. *Author*

Above left **DEVONSHIRE BANK:** Standard Class 4 2-6-0 No 76026 drifts down Devonshire Bank towards the site of the Victoria Brickworks with the 1.10pm from Bournemouth West on 18 July 1964. At Bath Green Park the train was taken forward to Bristol (Temple Meads) at 4.30pm by Standard Class 3 2-6-2 tank No 82036. *Author*

Above right **DEVONSHIRE BANK:** A little later on the same day Standard Class 5 4-6-0 No 73054 climbs out of Bath past the old Brickworks with the 3.35pm from Bristol (Temple Meads). No 73054 had taken over the train in Bath Green Park station, departing at 4.20pm. The train will arrive at Bournemouth West at 7.05pm. The green-liveried Class 5 had been at Green Park shed since April 1961. It was withdrawn from there in August 1965. *Author*

Left, right and below left
DEVONSHIRE BANK: Also photographed passing the former brickworks is ex-LMS Stanier 8F 2-8-0 No 48409 on the 11.00am goods from Bath to Evercreech Junction on 9 September 1964. The 8F, built at Swindon in 1943, had been allocated to Green Park shed the previous August, but was withdrawn in March 1965. As seen in the second picture, the train was banked in the rear by ex-GWR 0-6-0 pannier tank No 3742; also built at Swindon, in 1937, is it seen again in the third view as it returns to Bath after dropping back off the goods in Lyncombe Vale. It was the first ex-GWR engine to be based at Green Park in January 1959, and was withdrawn in November 1964. *Author*

Right **COMBE DOWN TUNNEL:** By 1965 four classes of BR Standard engine monopolised S&D line passenger trains. These were the Class 5 and Class 4 4-6-0s, 2-6-0s and 2-6-4 tanks. One of the latter, No 80037, emerges from Combe Down Tunnel with the 3.35pm train from Bristol Temple Meads to Bournemouth West on 11 May. The class had first appeared at Green Park in November 1963, having been displaced by dieselisation or electrification elsewhere on BR. By 1965 No 80037 was allocated to Templecombe, although its previous sheds had included Watford and Ashford (Kent). *Author*

Above **COMBE DOWN TUNNEL:** Despite the dominance of the Standard engines, other classes sometimes appeared on S&D line trains. In the spring of 1965 rebuilt Bulleid 'West Country' 'Pacific' No 34046 *Braunton* from Bournemouth shed was used on the 3.35pm Bristol Temple Meads to Bournemouth West train for several days, and is seen emerging from Combe Down Tunnel on 20 April 1965. After the loss of the 'Pines Express', the 4.20pm from Bath was the fastest train between Bath and Bournemouth, taking 2hr 45min with only an 8-minute wait at Templecombe. Following withdrawal, *Braunton* went to Barry scrapyard and was subsequently preserved. *Author*

Above: **MIDFORD:** Standard Class 4 2-6-0s had been associated with the S&D line since 1955, although none were ever based on it. During May 1965 No 76013 appeared regularly on the 1.10pm from Bournemouth West to Bristol Temple Meads, and is seen here approaching Midford with the train on 13 May. The three-coach train included a BR Mark I coach, topped and tailed by two of GWR origin. No 76013 was allocated to Bournemouth shed and withdrawn in September 1966. *Author*

Right: **MIDFORD:** Standard Class 4 4-6-0 No 75072 approaches Midford with the 4.35pm service from Green Park to Templecombe on 20 May 1965. This was one of three engines allocated new to Green Park in 1956 and with sister engine No 75073 it remained at Templecombe shed until December 1965. The third member of the class, No 75071, moved to BR(LMR) in 1964 and was withdrawn from Stoke-on-Trent shed in August 1967. No 75072 was fitted with a double chimney at Eastleigh Works in 1960. *Author*

No 48737 was allocated to Green Park shed at the end of 1963 while No 48309 arrived in August 1964. The two engines were withdrawn at the end of May 1965 and March 1966 respectively. No 48309 was later used on two of the special trains which ran on 1 & 2 January 1966 *Both author*

Above and right: **MIDFORD:** By 1965 the mainstay of freight traffic over the S&D line were the coal trains between Radstock and Portishead power station. The loaded trains were hauled to Bath by one of the shed's 8F 2-8-0s. (*above*) No 48737 drifts down towards Midford with empty coal wagons on 20 May 1965 while, No 48309 (*right*) heads a loaded coal train towards Midford Viaduct on 13 May 1965. The coal wagons were hauled to and from Portishead power station by another engine. For a brief period early in 1965 ex-GWR class 94XX Class pannier tanks were used on the Portishead trains.

THE FORMER MIDLAND LINE TO MANGOTSFIELD

From the winter of 1962 the former Midland line out of Bath saw an increasing number of its passenger trains to Bristol taken over by 'Peak' Class Type 4 diesel-electrics or, more occasionally, by DMUs. The 'Peaks', which were based at the new Bristol Bath Road diesel depot, were now hauling all the expresses between Bristol and Birmingham, and were used on the Bath trains as fill-in turns between their main-line duties. Freight still brought the occasional stranger into Bath, including 8F No 48163 in June 1965 (pictured overleaf), although the local goods yards on the line closed in July 1965.

Coal trains continued to run to Portishead Power Station, while some coal came from the north both to Bath gasworks and to the Co-op siding; the latter was situated just past the old Victoria Brickworks on the climb out of Bath on the S&D line. These two services continued for a time after passenger services were withdrawn on 6 March 1966 and the line to the south severed.

SALTFORD: Standard Class 5 4-6-0 No 73054 is seen again heading a short goods train near Saltford on the ex-Midland line to Bath Green Park on Thursday 3 June 1965. This was shortly before the local goods yards on the line closed. (Saltford's only station was on the ex-GWR main line. It closed in January 1970.). *Author*

SALTFORD: I had started the afternoon of Saturday 5 June 1965 next to the ex-GWR line from Bath Spa to Bristol. From my vantage point just west of Saltford I first saw across the fields an ex-LMS Stanier 8F 2-8-0 heading for Bath Green Park with a goods train, followed shortly afterwards by a 'Black 5' on a long rake of coaches. It looked as if I had 'missed the boat', but I moved over to the ex-Midland route in case something else unexpected should come along. Some time later the 8F, No 48163, passed light engine, the 'Black 5' followed shortly afterwards. It transpired that it had been delivering the empty stock for the Whit Monday special from Bath to Bournemouth West; this ran two days later on 7 June and was worked by Class 5 No 73051. A second special train, from Bristol to Bournemouth, ran on the same day. The final two Bank Holiday trains over the S&D ran to Bournemouth from Bath and Bristol respectively on August Bank Holiday 30 August 1965. *Author*

Inset **SALTFORD:** Although by the summer of 1965 several of the trains between Bristol (Temple Meads) and Bath Green Park were hauled by Type 4 'Peak' Class diesel-electrics (later Class 45), Standard Class 3 2-6-2 tanks were still well in evidence. Here No 82041 hurries the 3.35pm from Bristol (Temple Meads) to Bournemouth West past Saltford between Bitton and Bath on 5 June 1965. As noted previously, this train reversed at Bath Green Park and was taken on to Bournemouth by another engine. No. 82041 had been at Green Park shed since March 1959. *Author*

Below **BATH GREEN PARK:** On Saturday 30 October I spotted 'Black 5' No 44760 on the 1.10pm from Bournemouth West to Bristol Temple Meads at Green Park station. I managed to find a vantage point on what is now Windsor Bridge Road, opposite the gasworks. It was the last time I saw one of these engines in Bath. *Author*

Above **BITTON:** At the end of the summer of 1965 steam virtually disappeared from Bath Green Park to Bristol (Temple Meads) trains apart from on Saturdays. Several of the trains then reverted to steam haulage. Here Standard Class 3 2-6-2 tank No 82044 arrives at Bitton with the 11.40am from Bournemouth Central on Saturday 6 November. When Bournemouth West Station closed in October 1965, S&D line trains ran through to the Central Station. Since then the 11.40am from Bournemouth included three Bulleid coaches which had arrived earlier as part of a train from Waterloo. These returned to the capital that evening after arriving back in Bournemouth from Temple Meads. No 82044 was the last of the Class to be built at Swindon in August 1955. After spending time at Bristol Bath Road, Barrow Road and Taunton sheds it was withdrawn from Gloucester Horton Road in August 1965. It was reinstated in September for use from Bath Green Park but was finally withdrawn at the end of November. *Author*

BATH GREEN PARK: The use of Standard Class 3 tanks on trains to Bristol each Saturday continued until the end of 1965. Shortly before Christmas, No. 82041 waits at Green Park to take the11.40am from Bournemouth Central to Bristol (Temple Meads). No. 82041, also pictured on page 40, was allocated to Green Park in March 1959 and remained there until withdrawn at the end of December 1965. It was later cut up at Cashmore's scrapyard in Newport. *Author's collection*

THE LAST RITES AT BATH GREEN PARK JANUARY TO MARCH 1966

Saturday 1 and Sunday 2 January 1966

In the autumn of 1965 it was announced that all services to Bath Green Park were to be withdrawn on Monday 3 January 1966. However, due to problems with licensing of the alternative bus services, the closure had to be postponed and an emergency service introduced; nevertheless, two rail tours organised to 'celebrate' the closure on 1 and 2 January still ran. The LCGB's 'Mendip Merchantman' rail tour left Waterloo on the 1st behind 'Merchant Navy' 'Pacific' No 35011 *General Steam Navigation*. Although the class was officially barred from the S&D line, the train ran to Templecombe via Bournemouth. From Templecombe Ivatt Class 2 2-6-2 tanks Nos 41283 and 41307 took the rail tour on to Highbridge, where 9F 2-10-0 No 92243 took over for the run to Green Park via Bristol Temple Meads. Unfortunately the 9F failed at Warmley and the train had to be rescued by 8F 2-8-0 No 48760, which was waiting at Bath to haul it on to Templecombe. This it eventually did with sister engine No 48309. No 35011 then returned the train direct to Waterloo.

The RTCS's 'Somerset & Dorset' rail tour on the following day again made use of No 35011

BATH GREEN PARK: The two engines from the RTCS's 'Somerset & Dorset' rail tour, Class 'U' No 31639 and 'West Country' 'Pacific' No 34015 *Exmouth*, are serviced at Green Park shed on Sunday 2 January 1966 before returning south as light engines. *Author's collection*

General Steam Navigation. This time the 'Pacific' worked the train only as far as Broadstone, where it was replaced by unrebuilt 'West Country' 'Pacific' No 34015 *Exmouth* and ex-SR Class 'U' 2-6-0 No 31639, which brought it into Bath. There 8F No 48309 took over for the run to Highbridge via Bristol Temple Meads. At Highbridge Nos 41283 and 41307 were waiting to return the train to Templecombe. No 35011 again hauled the train back to Waterloo.

BATH GREEN PARK: From Bath the 'Somerset & Dorset' rail tour was hauled to Highbridge via Bristol Temple Meads by No 48309. The train is seen leaving Green Park station. The passengers would no doubt have welcomed the steam heating with which the 8F was fitted. *Author's collection*

Saturday 5 and Sunday 6 March 1966

The timetable for the emergency service that BR(WR) was forced to introduce from Green Park from Monday 3 January was a meagre one, with just four trains to Templecombe and two to Bristol Temple Meads. The only through train in either direction between Bournemouth and Bath was the 6.10pm from Bournemouth Central. The Bristol trains were both diesel-worked but the S&D trains remained steam-hauled until closure. This was finally fixed for Monday 7 March 1966.

To mark the event two special trains ran on both Saturday 5 and Sunday 6 March. On the Saturday the GWR Society ran a special from Bath Green Park to Bournemouth Central and back behind 8F No 48706, while the LCGB organised a rerun of its January 'Somerset & Dorset' rail tour. This left Waterloo for Templecombe behind the now preserved 'Merchant Navy' 'Pacific' No 35028 *Clan Line*. Ivatt Class 2 2-6-2 tanks Nos 41249 and 41307 then took the train to Highbridge and back to Evercreech Junction. From Evercreech Junction it was taken over the Mendips to Bath by two unrebuilt 'Pacifics', 'West Country' No 34015 *Exmouth* and 'Battle of Britain' No 34057 *Biggin Hill*. The two engines later returned the rail tour to Bournemouth, where No 35028 was waiting for the run back to Waterloo. Later that day No 41249 worked the 4.00pm service from Highbridge to Templecombe, the last public train to leave the S&D station there. That evening No 80043 and sister engine No 80041 headed the last public train, the 6.10pm from Bournemouth Central to *Continued on Page 47...*

BATH GREEN PARK: The SLS special is seen waiting to leave Bath Green Park behind 8F 2-8-0 No 48706 and Class 4 2-6-4 tank No 80043 on Sunday 6 March 1966. On its return it became the last train ever to arrive at the station. *M. E. J. Deane collection, courtesy of Ian Bennett*

Right **BATH GREEN PARK:** 'West Country' 'Pacific' No 34013 *Okehampton* and 'Battle of Britain' 'Pacific' No 34057 *Biggin Hill* head out of Bath with the RCTS special. It was the last ever passenger train to climb Devonshire Bank and over the Mendips to Templecombe. *Author*

Below **MIDFORD:** Unrebuilt 'Battle of Britain' 'Pacific' No 34057 *Biggin Hill* drifts through Midford to work the RCTS's 'Somerset & Dorset Farewell Rail Tour' from Green Park to Templecombe on Sunday 6 March 1966. *Author's collection*

BATH GREEN PARK: The delay in closing the lines to Green Park had thwarted BR(WR)'s plans to rid itself of steam at the end of 1965, if only by two months! On the closure of the line all of its steam engines were withdrawn. The last of them, seen stored at a deserted Bath Green Park shed awaiting disposal in the spring of 1966, were Ivatt tanks Nos 41307, 41290 and 41223, together with 'Jinty' tank No 47276. The latter, the last ex-LMS engine at Bath, was briefly in the limelight in September 1965 when, painted green on one side only, it was used in the feature film *The Wrong Box. Author's collection*

... Continued from Page 44
Bath Green Park, out of Templecombe. The train arrived at Bath, rather later than scheduled, to the sound of exploding detonators.

Next day, Sunday 6 March, 8F No 48706 and Standard Class 4 2-6-4 tank No 80043 were waiting at Green Park to work the Stephenson Locomotive Society's 'Last passenger train from Bath, Templecombe and Bournemouth'. Many of its passengers arrived at Green Park from the Midlands and in a chartered DMU. After arrival at Templecombe, the SLS special was drawn back out of the station in the time-honoured manner by Ivatt tank No 41249 before proceeding to Bournemouth Central.

The second special on the Sunday was the RCTS's 'Somerset & Dorset Farewell Rail Tour'. *Clan Line* again headed the train between Waterloo and Templecombe, this time via Bournemouth Central. Ivatt tanks Nos 41249 and 41283 then hauled the train from Templecombe to Highbridge, where rebuilt 'West Country' 'Pacific' No 34013 *Okehampton* was waiting to haul it up the main line, through Bristol Temple Meads, to Mangotsfield. There 'Hymek' No D7014 replaced it for the run into Green Park. Meanwhile 'Battle of Britain' 'Pacific' No 34057 *Biggin Hill* had run light to Bath to work the special back to Templecombe. At Bath *Biggin Hill* was joined by *Okehampton*, which had turned on the triangle at Mangotsfield and run light to Green Park. The two engines then became the last to haul a passenger train out of Green Park station over the S&D line. The last arrival at Green Park was the returning SLS special from Bournemouth, while the last departure of all was its chartered DMU back to Birmingham New Street.

BLUE ANCHOR (WSR): Since its closure the Somerset & Dorset Joint Railway has been celebrated during many heritage railway galas. The 50th anniversary of its closure was marked by a major event at the West Somerset Railway. Here preserved S&D 7F 2-8-0 No 53808 is seen at Blue Anchor with a train from Bishops Lydeard to Minehead duing the event on 5 March 2016. Steam has also returned to Bath Spa in recent years on various special trains. *Steve Edge*

Index to locations & locomotives